WARRIORS

SAMURAI

Deborah Murrell

QEB Publishing

Copyright © QEB Publishing, Inc. 2009

Published in the United States by
QEB Publishing, Inc.
3 Wrigley, Suite A
Irvine, CA 92618

www.qeb-publishing.com

Library of Congress Cataloging-in-
Publication Data

Murrell, Deborah Jane, 1963-
Samurai / by Deborah Murrell.
     p. cm. -- (QEB warriors)
Includes index.
ISBN 978-1-59566-734-2 (hardcover)
1. Samurai--Juvenile literature. 2. Military
art and science--Japan--Juvenile literature. 3.
Japan--History, Military--Juvenile literature.
I. Title.
DS827.S3M875 2010
355.00952--dc22

2009003545

Printed and bound in China

Author Deborah Murrell
Consultant Philip Steele
Project Editor Eve Marleau
Designer and
     Picture Researcher Andrew McGovern
Illustrator Peter Dennis

Publisher Steve Evans
Creative Director Zeta Davies
Managing Editor Amanda Askew

Picture credits
Key: t=top, b=bottom, r=right, l=left, c=centre
Alamy 5b Alan King engraving, 13tr blickwinkel/
McPHOTO/MKD, 23b Mary Evans Picture Library,
27b JTB Photo, 29t Jon Arnold
Bridgeman 4, 6 Pat Nicolle, 10r Ogata Gekko,
12t Dan Escott, 12b Pat Nicolle, 15l Japanese School,
20 HM Burton, 22 English School, 25t Tsukioka
Yoshitoshi, 25b Japanese School
Corbis 9r Asian Art & Archaeology, 11b Asian Art &
Archaeology, 17t, 19t Burstein Collection, 26t Alinari
Archives, 27t Bettmann, 29b Roger Ressmeyer
Getty Images 16–17 AFP, 28r Karin Slade
Photolibrary 11t JTB Photo, 24l JTB Photo,
26b The Print Collector
Shutterstock 15b Radu Razvan
Topfoto 5t Ancient Art & Architecture Collection,
13l Werner Forman Archive, 13r Werner Forman
Archive, 14r Werner Forman Archive, 15c Werner
Forman Archive, 23t Topham Picturepoint &
Warner Bros

The words in **bold** are explained
in the glossary on page 30.

CONTENTS

What was a samurai? 4

When did samurai live? 6

Becoming a samurai. 8

The pen and the sword 10

Weapons. 12

Armor 14

Ninja 16

Early clans 18

The rise of the samurai 20

Samurai in battle 22

Three great men 24

The last shoguns 26

The decline of samurai 28

Glossary 30

Index 32

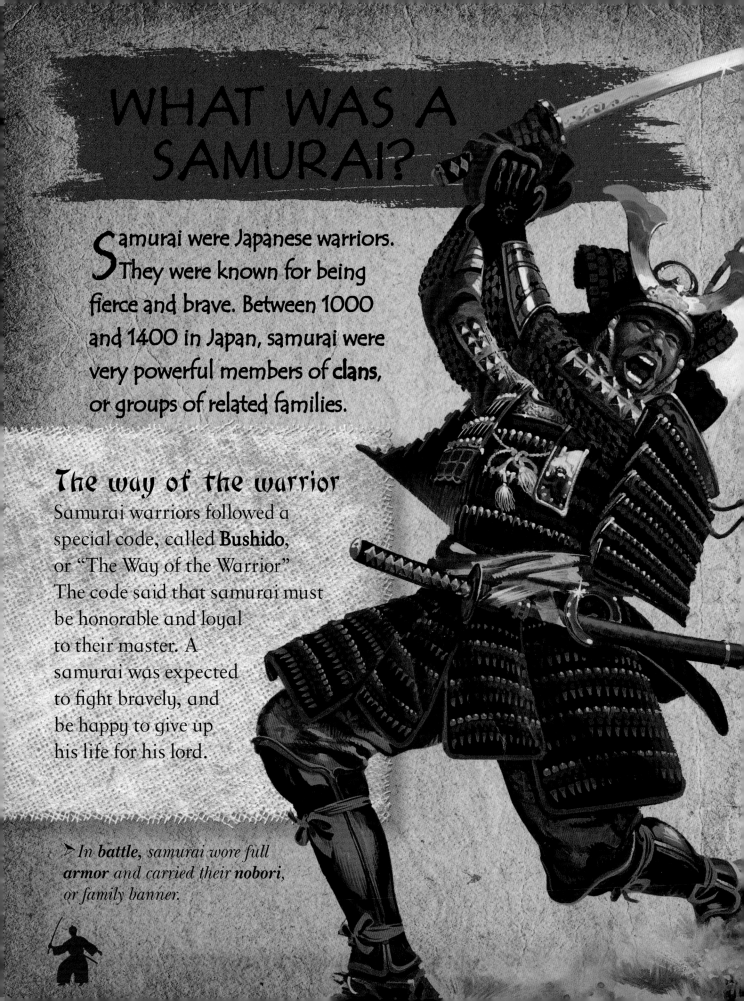

WHAT WAS A SAMURAI?

Samurai were Japanese warriors. They were known for being fierce and brave. Between 1000 and 1400 in Japan, samurai were very powerful members of **clans**, or groups of related families.

The way of the warrior

Samurai warriors followed a special code, called **Bushido**, or "The Way of the Warrior" The code said that samurai must be honorable and loyal to their master. A samurai was expected to fight bravely, and be happy to give up his life for his lord.

➤ *In **battle**, samurai wore full **armor** and carried their **nobori**, or family banner.*

The First Emperor

In Japanese myth, the Sun goddess Amaterasu sent her grandson from Heaven to Earth to be the first emperor of Japan.

Family pride

Samurai were very proud of their family history. Many came from families that had been warriors for several generations, though others were only just learning Bushido. A samurai told stories of his family's bravery to the warrior he was about to fight. He also had his family's history written on a banner, which he carried to war.

➤ *Samurai sometimes carried fans called "tessen". They had iron spikes and could be used as weapons.*

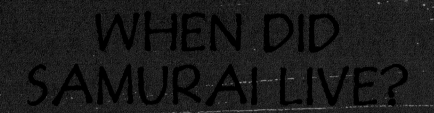

Samurai were powerful in Japan from about 1000 to the late 1800s. Early samurai were warriors on horseback. From the early 1600s, samurai were important in government, so they spent less time fighting. They also studied art and **literature**.

Social classes

Japan had a feudal system. People were in classes, or groups, depending on how important they were. Everyone was loyal to the emperor, but the **Bushi**, or samurai class, were in charge of running the country, so they ruled the lower classes.

▼For a samurai on horseback, the most important weapon was a a bow.

The first samurai

For hundreds of years, Japan was divided into **regions** controlled by clans who fought each other for power. Eventually, one clan, the Yamato, became the most powerful in Japan. The clan asked other clan leaders to fight for it. These clan leaders were the first samurai warriors.

Hokkaidō

JAPAN

Sado

Sea Of Japan

Kanazawa ●

Oki

Edo (Tokyo) ●

Korea Strait

Kyoto ●

Osaka ●

Honshu

Tsushima

Yamaguchi ●

PACIFIC OCEAN

Shikoku

Nagasaki ● ● Shimabara
Gota Islands

Kyushu

East China Sea

⌃ *Today, the capital city of Japan is Tokyo. In medieval Japan, Tokyo was called Edo.*

WARRIOR WISDOM

The word "samurai" means "those who serve". In the 900s, only men in the capital city, Kyoto, who served the emperor were called samurai. Later, any soldiers serving a powerful landlord were called samurai.

BECOMING A SAMURAI

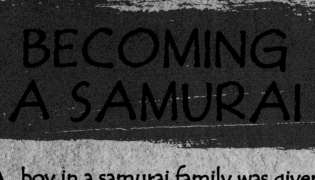

A boy in a samurai family was given his first sword when he was born. This was not a real sword, but a symbol of the life he was going to lead. When he was about 13 years old, he was given a proper sword, armor and a warrior name. Half of this name was his father's name, and the other half was his own.

Stages of training

Samurai boys were brought up not to fear death or danger. They began training at three years old with their father, using wooden swords. They were given real weapons at 13 years old and sent to a relative or **fencing** teacher. They were in training until they were 20 years old.

It was important for samurai boys to practice their sword skills.

Warrior woman

Tomoe Gozen (c.1157–1247) was a female samurai. She fought alongside her husband, Minamoto no Yoshinaka, and was a great swordswoman and **archer**.

Girls and women

The wives and daughters of samurai were expected to look after the home. Girls learned to handle money and run the household. Female samurai warriors, such as Tomoe Gozen, were rare.

THE PEN AND THE SWORD

S amurai were expected to be able to read and write as well as they could fight. Warriors who could do both well were admired. When they were not fighting, samurai studied culture and the arts.

櫻ノ詩 兒島髙德

Inspirational art

Samurai were often the subject of paintings. Images of heroes or imaginary great warriors helped samurai to remember the bravery of others and to follow Bushido.

➢ *The samurai Kojima no Takanori writes a poem on a cherry tree.*

Fighting talk

The Heike Monogatari, or Tale of the Heike, is a collection of stories about two clans, the Taira and Minamoto. Samurai studied these stories because the heroes of the stories were seen as good examples for samurai to follow.

➤ *The battles between the Taira and Minamoto clans were known as the Gempei War.*

Taira no Tadamori

Taira no Tadamori (1096–1153) was a very important samurai, famous for both his writing and fighting skills. He was said to have been the first warrior to serve the emperor at court.

WEAPONS

Samurai had many different weapons. When they were on horseback, samurai fought with a bow, so they could fire arrows at the enemy from far away. They also carried a long and a short sword, and sometimes a dagger and spear.

➤ *Samurai on horseback used a bow and arrows when charging into battle.*

Long sword

The **katana** was a long, curved sword. It had a single-edged blade and a long handle so that it could be held with two hands for extra power. Bushido said that the katana was like the warrior's soul. Samurai often gave their katana a name.

➤ *Samurai who fought on foot used their katana swords.*

◄ These arrows were used by samurai in the 1300s.

Short sword

The **wakizashi** sword was shorter than the katana sword. Together, these two swords were called the **daisho**, which means "big and small".

➤ Samurai kept the wakizashi sword with them at all times —they even slept with it!

➤ A tsuba, or hand guard, stopped the samurai's hand from slipping onto the sword's blade.

Bow and arrows

A bow and arrows were the most useful weapons a samurai on horseback could have. Bows were about 8 feet (2.5 meters) long and made of silk and bamboo. Arrows had sharp spikes at the end.

WARRIOR WISDOM

In 1867, samurai were banned from carrying swords. However, many samurai started to carry their swords secretly. They even hid them in walking sticks!

ARMOR

T he style of armor worn by samurai warriors changed over the centuries. However, the various pieces of samurai armor were always more or less the same.

Helmet

Shoulder guard

Chest armor

Arm guard

Body armor

On the top half of their body, samurai wore a helmet, shoulder guards, chest armor and one or two arm guards. Their thighs were protected by an apron, or skirt, made of armor. The bottom of their legs was covered by armor that looked like shin pads. They also wore animal skin boots with splints made of brass to protect the feet.

Apron

Animal skin boot

➤ A suit of samurai armor from the 1500s or 1600s.

Helmets

Samurai helmets were designed not only for protection but also to give the warrior a frightening appearance. Sometimes samurai also wore a metal face **mask**, which must have made them look terrifying.

◄ *A helmet decorated with a war fan. Samurai used fans for signaling and sending commands.*

▲ *Decorations on top of helmets made it easy to recognize samurai on the battlefield.*

The Red Devils

The samurai, Li Naomasa, had the armor of all his troops colored red. This made it easy to recognize each other, and also scared the enemy. Soon they were known as "The Red Devils".

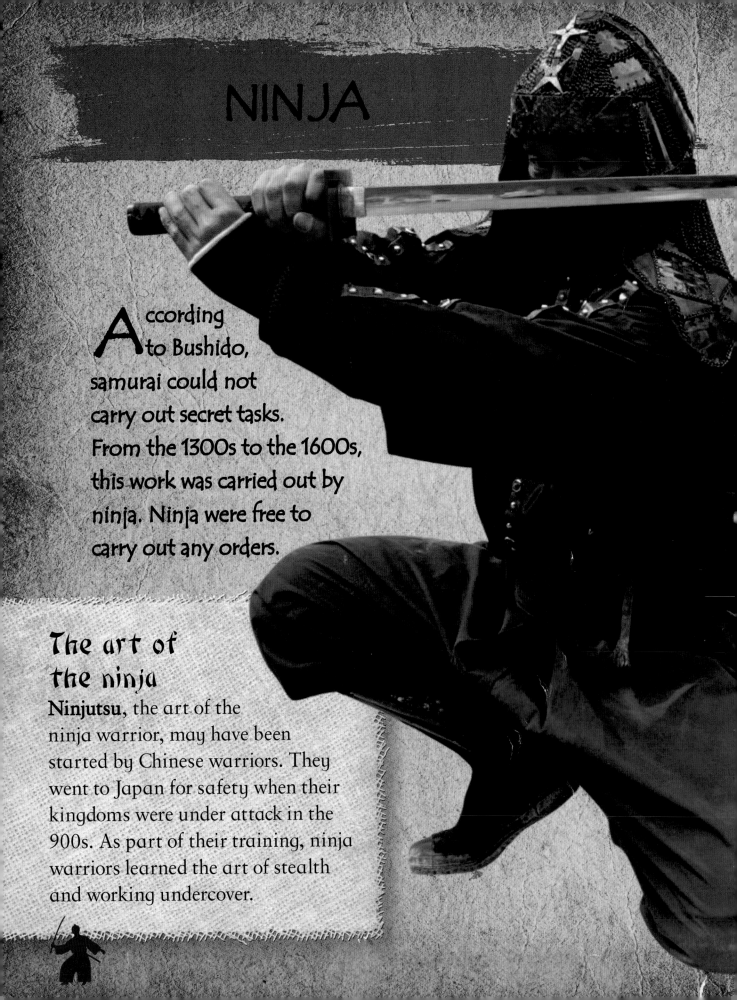

NINJA

According to Bushido, samurai could not carry out secret tasks. From the 1300s to the 1600s, this work was carried out by ninja. Ninja were free to carry out any orders.

The art of the ninja

Ninjutsu, the art of the ninja warrior, may have been started by Chinese warriors. They went to Japan for safety when their kingdoms were under attack in the 900s. As part of their training, ninja warriors learned the art of stealth and working undercover.

Ninja in films

Japanese ninja have appeared in many feature films, including *Teenage Mutant Ninja Turtles* and James Bond films. In *You Only Live Twice* (1967), James trains at a ninja camp in Japan.

Now you see them, now you don't

Ninja were so good at hiding and surprising an enemy that some people believed that they could become invisible, or turn themselves into animals. A ninja often wore a **shoku** on each hand. This was an iron band that went around the hand, with spikes on the inside.

◄ *People believed that ninja had special powers because they were so good at hiding from enemies.*

▲ *Shoku helped ninja to block swords and climb trees like a cat.*

EARLY CLANS

By the 1000s, there were two very powerful family groupings in Japan. They were the Taira and the Minamoto clans. These families fought each other in the Gempei War.

Taira strength

After beating the Minamoto clan in 1160, Taira no Kiyomori became the first warrior to be given the job of adviser to the emperor. He eventually took control of the **government** for himself. His clan ruled through the emperor, rather than by themselves.

Minamoto no Yoritomo

In 1192, Minamoto no Yoritomo took the title of **shogun**. A shogun was a samurai military leader. Yorimoto decided that a samurai could only become a shogun if his father had been one before him.

*◄ The warrior **monk**, Benkei, led the Minamoto clan to battle in the Gempei War.*

Gempei War

In the Heiji Rebellion of 1160, the Taira beat the Minamoto clan in battle. Their victory did not last long. In 1180, the Minamoto returned and beat the Taira clan. This was the first battle of the Gempei War.

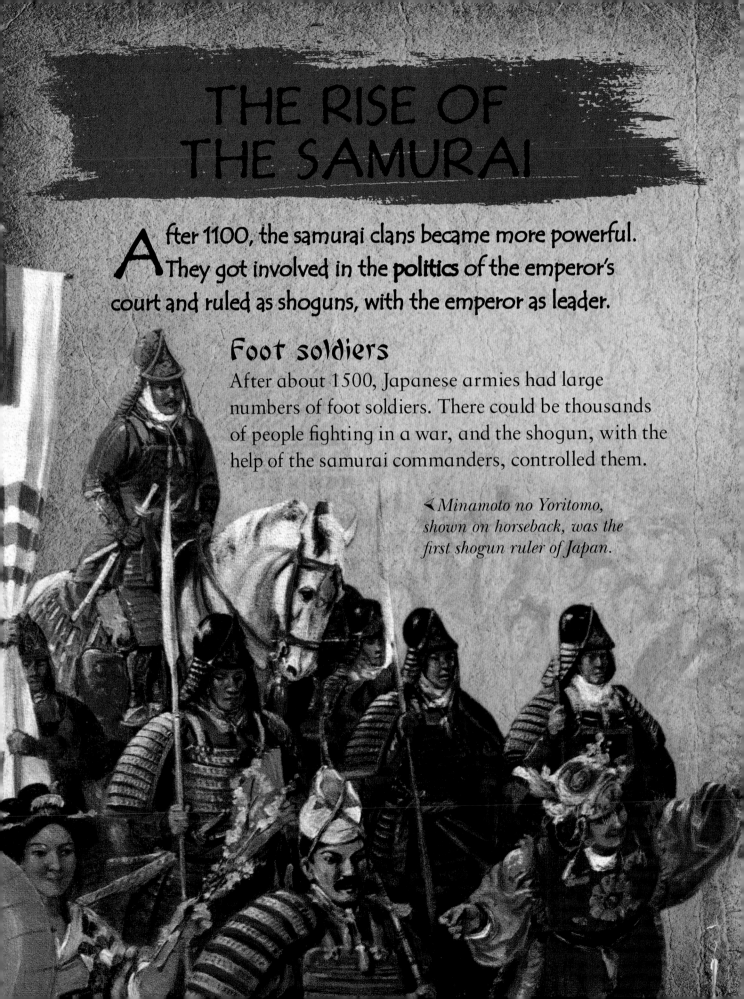

THE RISE OF THE SAMURAI

After 1100, the samurai clans became more powerful. They got involved in the **politics** of the emperor's court and ruled as shoguns, with the emperor as leader.

Foot soldiers

After about 1500, Japanese armies had large numbers of foot soldiers. There could be thousands of people fighting in a war, and the shogun, with the help of the samurai commanders, controlled them.

◄ *Minamoto no Yoritomo, shown on horseback, was the first shogun ruler of Japan.*

Ruling classes

The samurai had a lot of power in Japan. They had a great deal of control over the lives of people from the lower classes. After about 1500, a law made it illegal for anyone except samurai to carry weapons. This stopped the lower classes from rebelling against them.

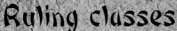

▼Samurai were powerful and well respected by the lower classes in Japan.

WARRIOR WISDOM

In the late 1000s, the samurai Kamakura Kagemasa was shot in the right eye by an arrow. To remove the arrow, a friend needed to put his foot on Kagemasa's face. This would have been a great dishonor, so he refused.

SAMURAI IN BATTLE

In battle, samurai often fought on horseback as well as on foot. Samurai attacked in groups led by one man. They followed the unit's nobori, or banner.

Charge!

Samurai on horseback were terrifying. When a battle was going well, a samurai army might break into a charge, chasing the enemy off the battlefield.

> ➤ *Samurai always carried the nobori into battle.*

The Last Samurai

The 2003 film, *The Last Samurai*, starring Tom Cruise, is about a soldier who visits Japan after the emperor returns to rule. He meets a rebel group of samurai warriors and lives among them to learn samurai ways.

➤ *One-on-one fights are called* **duels**. *These fights were usually to settle an argument.*

Revenge

Samurai sometimes challenged each other to a fight, especially if one of the samurai wanted to take revenge against the other. He might want to fight the son of a warrior who had killed his own father.

THREE GREAT MEN

Between 1400 and 1600, different states of Japan were at war with each other. This was called the Warring States Period. Three samurai leaders managed to make the country one again. They called themselves **daimyo**, or "great names".

Oda Nobunaga (1534-1582)

One of the most powerful daimyo was Oda Nobunaga. He defeated the rulers of Kyoto and took over the city in 1568. Hideyoshi and Ieyasu were his followers.

⌃ *Oda Nobunaga tried to unite Japan under one ruler, but he died before he could succeed.*

WARRIOR WISDOM

The family of shoguns called the Tokugawa made sure the other daimyo stayed loyal, by putting them in charge of their own lands. The daimyo lived in their castle towns, but their families lived in Edo, the capital city. Each daimyo only met his family once a year when he marched to Edo to pay respect to the shogun.

Toyotomi Hideyoshi (1536-1598)

Toyotomi Hideyoshi was one of Oda Nobunaga's most trusted men. When he heard that Nobunaga had been killed, Hideyoshi began to take control. By 1591, he ruled a large part of Japan. As he was not from the Minamoto family, he could not call himself a shogun. However, when he died, his five-year-old son became ruler.

⋀ *Hideyoshi blows on a conch shell trumpet to signal to his people.*

Tokugawa Ieyasu (1542-1616)

After the death of Hideyoshi, some people were happy with his son as ruler, but others were not. These people supported Tokugawa Ieyasu. The two sides fought at Sekigahara in 1600, and Ieyasu won. As he was from the Minamoto family, he named himself shogun.

⋖ *Tokugawa Ieyasu was named shogun in 1603. From then on, Tokugawa shoguns ruled Japan until the mid-1800s.*

THE LAST SHOGUNS

In 1639, the shogun banned trade with European countries. Japan only began to trade with Europe again in the 1800s. Many samurai did not like this, and wanted to remove the Tokugawa shogun who allowed it. They succeeded, and in 1868, Emperor Meiji became Japan's new ruler.

◄ *Tokugawa Yoshinobu was Japan's last shogun.*

Emperor Meiji's army

Almost as soon as Meiji took control, he stripped the shoguns of all their power. Meiji also thought that a modern army, such as the armies of Europe, would be better than the samurai system. He even encouraged foreign trade. This annoyed the samurai who had made him ruler.

➤ *Emperor Meiji was also known as Mutsuhito.*

Western samurai

Few men from the west were allowed to be samurai, but at least two western sailors were made samurai by Shogun Tokugawa. One was the English adventurer, William Adams (1564–1620). He was given the daisho swords and called Miura Anjin.

Kumamoto Castle

The daimyo of Satsuma had a strong army, armed with both samurai swords and guns. They decided to challenge Emperor Meiji. In 1877, they attacked one of the emperor's most important castles, Kumamoto. After a long battle, Emperor Meiji's army beat the samurai.

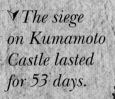

▼ *The siege on Kumamoto Castle lasted for 53 days.*

THE DECLINE OF SAMURAI

Samurai became less powerful after the 1600s because guns began to be used in Japan. The defeat of the Satsuma Rebellion made them lose even more faith in their strength. Although samurai clans still existed, they never regained the power that they once had.

Osaka Castle

Osaka Castle was the home of the Toyotomi clan. Tokugawa Ieyasu had been shogun since 1603, but in 1614 he still feared the Toyotomi clan, so he attacked Osaka Castle. For days, Ieyasu fired cannon at the walls and, eventually, Hideyori Toyotomi signed a peace **treaty**, or agreement. Soon after, the fighting began again. Osaka Castle was finally taken over in June 1615, and the Tokugawa clan continued to rule Japan for more than two centuries. Today, the castle has been rebuilt. It is seen as a symbol of the great power and bravery of the samurai.

⌃ *Osaka Castle was built high up on stone to protect it from attackers.*

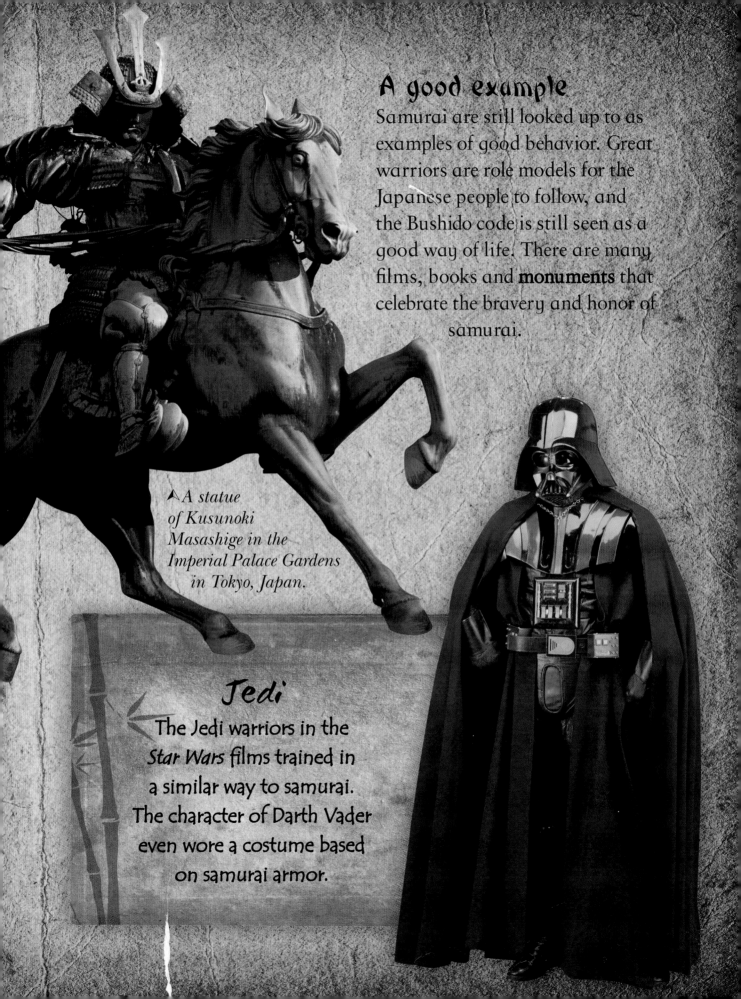

A good example

Samurai are still looked up to as examples of good behavior. Great warriors are role models for the Japanese people to follow, and the Bushido code is still seen as a good way of life. There are many films, books and **monuments** that celebrate the bravery and honor of samurai.

▲ *A statue of Kusunoki Masashige in the Imperial Palace Gardens in Tokyo, Japan.*

Jedi

The Jedi warriors in the *Star Wars* films trained in a similar way to samurai. The character of Darth Vader even wore a costume based on samurai armor.

GLOSSARY

Archer A soldier who fights with a bow and arrows.

Armor Protective clothing, usually made of metal or leather.

Battle A fight between two groups of people.

Bushi The social class of samurai and their families.

Bushido A code of behavior that samurai were supposed to follow.

Clan A group of closely related families.

Daimyo The head of a great family in Japan.

Daisho The two swords (the katana and wakizashi) that samurai traditionally carried.

Duel A fight between two people, usually with swords.

Emperor The ruler of an empire. An empire is a large number of states ruled over by one person, a group of people or another state.

Fencing The practice of sword-fighting.

Government A group of people who rule a country or state.

Katana A long, curved sword that samurai used as a weapon.

Literature Written work such as poems and stories.

Mask Something that covers the face to hide it or for protection.

Monk A man who is part of a religious group that lives separately from everyone else.

Monument A building, statue or other structure that is often built in memory of something.

Ninjutsu The art of the ninja warrior.

Nobori The banner of a group of warriors led by a shogun.

Politics The beliefs and ideas of people about how to rule a country or run a government.

Region An area in a country or state.

Shogun A samurai commander.

Shoku An iron band with spikes worn on the hand by ninja.

Treaty An agreement between two groups of people.

Wakizashi A short sword that samurai used as a weapon.

INDEX

archers 9, 30
armor 4, 8, 14–15, 30

bows and arrows 12, 13, 21, 30
Bushi class 6, 30
Bushido code 4, 5, 10, 12, 16, 29, 30

clans 4, 7, 18, 28, 30

daimyo leaders 24, 27, 30
daisho swords 27, 30

families 4, 5, 8, 18, 24, 25
fans 5, 15
feudal system 6

Gempei War 11, 18, 19
government 6, 18, 30
guns 27, 28

Heiji Rebellion 19
Heike Monogatari 11
helmets 14, 15
Hideyori Toyotomi 28

katana sword 12, 31
Kumamoto Castle 27

Meiji, Emperor 26, 27
Minamoto clan 11, 18, 19, 25
Minomoto no Yoritomo 11, 20

Ninja warriors 16–17
nobori banner 4, 5, 22, 31

Oda Nobunaga 24, 25
Osaka Castle 28

Satsuma Rebellion 27, 28
shoguns 19, 20, 24, 25, 26–27, 28, 31
spears 12
swords 8, 9, 12, 13, 27, 30, 31

Taira clan 11, 18, 19
Taira no Kiyomori 18
Tokugawa Ieyasu 25, 28
Tokugawa shoguns 24, 25, 26, 27, 28
Tokugawa Yoshinobu 26
Toyotomi clan 28
Toyotomi Hideyoshi 25
training 9, 16

wakizashi sword 13, 31
Warring States Period 24
weapons 6, 9, 12–13, 21
women 9

Yamato clan 7